Walruses

by Martha E. H. Rustad

Consulting Editor: Gail Saunders-Smith, Ph.D.

Consultant: Jody Rake, Science Writer,
SeaWorld Education Department

Pebble Books

an imprint of Capstone Press
Mankato, Minnesota

Pebble Books are published by Capstone Press
151 Good Counsel Drive, P.O. Box 669, Mankato, Minnesota 56002
http://www.capstone-press.com

1 2 3 4 5 6 08 07 06 05 04 03

Library of Congress Cataloging-in-Publication Data
Rustad, Martha E. H. (Martha Elizabeth Hillman), 1975–
Walruses / by Martha Rustad.
p. cm.—(Ocean life)
Summary: Simple text and photographs describe the physical characteristics
and behavior of walruses.
Includes bibliographical references (p. 23) and index.
ISBN 0-7368-1659-3 (hardcover)
1. Walrus—Juvenile literature. [1. Walrus.] I. Title. II. Series.
QL737.P62 R87 2003
599.79′9—dc21   2002014778

Note to Parents and Teachers

The Ocean Life series supports national science standards for units on the diversity and unity of life. The series shows that animals have features that help them live in different environments. This book describes walruses and illustrates how they live. The photographs support early readers in understanding the text. The repetition of words and phrases helps early readers learn new words. This book also introduces early readers to subject-specific vocabulary words, which are defined in the Words to Know section. Early readers may need assistance to read some words and to use the Table of Contents, Words to Know, Read More, Internet Sites, and Index/Word List sections of the book.

Table of Contents

Walruses. 5

Body 11

What Walruses Do 19

Words to Know 22

Read More 23

Internet Sites. 23

Index/Word List. 24

Walruses are mammals.

Walruses live in herds.

Walruses swim in the ocean. They rest on land and on ice.

Walruses have blubber
to keep them warm.

Walruses have
hairy, wrinkled skin.

tusks

Walruses have two tusks.

flippers

flippers

Walruses have four flippers.

whiskers

Walruses have whiskers. They use their whiskers to find clams and snails to eat.

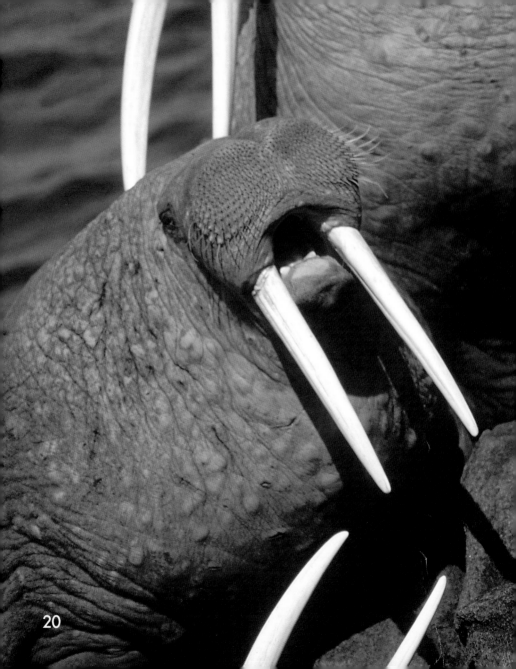

Walruses bellow.

Words to Know

bellow—to shout or to roar

blubber—fat under the skin of some animals

clam—a small ocean animal that lives inside a shell; clamshells are hard to open.

flipper—a flat limb with bones found on a sea animal; flippers help walruses swim in the ocean and walk on ice and land.

herd—a large group of animals; walrus herds have as many as 1,000 walruses.

mammal—a warm-blooded animal with a backbone; mammals feed milk to their young.

tusk—a long, curved, pointed tooth; walruses use their tusks for protection and to pull themselves up on the ice.

whisker—a long, stiff hair near the mouth of some animals; walruses have very sensitive whiskers that they use to find food.

wrinkled—covered with creases or lines; thick, wrinkled skin helps protect walruses from the tusks of other walruses.

Read More

Murray, Julie. *Walruses.* Animal Kingdom. Edina, Minn.: Abdo, 2002.

Rotter, Charles. *Walruses.* Naturebooks. Chanhassen, Minn.: Child's World, 2001.

Staub, Frank J. *Walruses.* Early Bird Nature Books. Minneapolis: Lerner Publications, 1999.

Internet Sites

Track down many sites about walruses.
Visit the FACT HOUND at *http://www.facthound.com*

IT IS EASY! IT IS FUN!

1) Go to *http://www.facthound.com*
2) Type in: 0736816593

3) Click on "FETCH IT" and FACT HOUND will find several links hand-picked by our editors.

Relax and let our pal FACT HOUND do the research for you!

Index/Word List

bellow, 21
blubber, 11
clams, 19
eat, 19
flippers, 17
four, 17
hairy, 13
herds, 7

ice, 9
land, 9
live, 7
mammals, 5
ocean, 9
rest, 9
skin, 13
snails, 19

swim, 9
tusks, 15
two, 15
warm, 11
whiskers, 19
wrinkled, 13

Word Count: 55
Early-Intervention Level: 9

Credits

Steve Christensen, cover designer and illustrator; Patrick D. Dentinger, production designer; Kelly Garvin, photo researcher

Corbis/Robert Holmes, 4; W. Perry Conway, 14
Digital Stock/Animals & Wildlife, cover
Images International/Bud Nielsen, 20
Minden Pictures/Flip Nicklin, 10
Tom Stack & Associates/Thomas Kitchin, 1, 12; Mark Newman, 6; Jeff Foott, 8; Tom Stack, 18
U.S. Fish & Wildlife Service/Bill Hickey, 16